THE SHEARERS

SONS
1386

THE SHEARERS | ANDREW CHAPMAN

For Josie

A Lothian Book

Published in Australia and New Zealand in 2006
by Hachette Livre Australia Pty Ltd
Level 17, 207 Kent Street, Sydney NSW 2000
www.hachette.com.au

Aboriginal and Torres Strait Islander people are warned that this book contains some images of people who are now deceased.

National Library of Australia
Cataloguing-in-Publication data:

Chapman, Andrew Lachlan.
The shearers.

ISBN 0 7344 0834 X.

1. Sheep-shearing – Australia – Pictorial works. 2. Sheep shearers (Persons) – Australia – Pictorial works. 3. Country life – Australia – Pictorial works. 4. Australia – Pictorial works. I. Title.

636.30833

Cover photograph: Peter 'Walkabout' Stewart, Mallawa Shed, Maude, NSW
Frontispiece: Old Cooinbil Shed, Coleambally, NSW

Designed by Phil Campbell
Printed and bound in China by Imago Productions

THE SHEARERS

Standing on the banks of the Murrumbidgee, one of our great inland rivers, steeped in the histories of both black and white settlement in Australia, I'm looking back towards the old shearers' quarters that grace the river near Hay in southwestern New South Wales. These inland rivers were the first highways that helped build Australia's great wool industry.

It's hot—bloody hot—about 40 degrees these last few days. The nights aren't much better either and while being grateful to our host for allowing us to stay in the shearers' corrugated-iron quarters, the heat drives me to slip into the cool waters of the Murrumbidgee. As I float around I look back on the shearing shed and quarters and reflect on the hard lives of the shearers and why I like photographing their lifestyle.

I've travelled to these semi-arid areas of Australia to photograph the big shearing sheds and the people who inhabit them, to wait and to capture what I once thought was a dying way of life. I'm still waiting for shearing to die out, superceded by some you-beaut robot technology or chemical fleecing, but I've been expecting these changes since I first heard about them, way back in the 1970s. Apart from a few luxuries like back slings and electric fans, most shearers work the same way they always have done … the hard way.

Down dusty tracks and along riverbanks, the great properties are still there, steeped in history: Toganmain, Mungadal, Pevensey, Isis Downs and many others are a living testament to the past. Baked by a ferocious summer sun, blown by the cold winds, survivors of occasional floods, droughts and fires, some eaten by termites, these sheds somehow last to face another shearing season. Inside, shafts of light across lanolin-encrusted timber create rich, ageing patterns of beauty. The soft sounds of a working shed and the hum of the shearers' cutters is broken only by the occasional bleat or kicking of hooves and the muttered swearing of a shearer, whose only intent is to get through the next run.

Shearing must be the most labour-intensive, hot, dusty, sweaty work a person can do. It takes a special sort of person to be a shearer. The love of a knockabout lifestyle and a devil-may-care attitude often masks a deep respect for the history and craft of shearing. As always, today's shearers are super fit and do it hard, working a full eight hours in back-breaking positions, often in rudimentary sheds where the mercury can creep into the mid to high forties. Shearing a hundred and fifty to three hundred-plus sheep is as hard a day's work as you can get. One shearer I spoke to can recall seeing men collapse when shed temperatures reached into the fifties.

In some ways today's shearers are better off than their forebears, who often had to walk from shed to shed. It was not unknown for a shearer to die along the track when a creek or waterhole didn't materialise. Shearing by blade with no electric fans for cooling, in crowded sheds of perhaps sixty or more shearers with supporting roustabouts, cooks, classers and farmhands seeing the numbers grow into the hundreds. With no fresh fruit and vegetables in the diet, it was mutton, spuds and onions, black tea and scones, no cold beer, but the odd bottle of rum.

Today the shearing teams turn up to the sheds in Holden utes and Ford panelvans, often bringing an air-conditioner to fit into the tin box of a bedroom that will become home for the next few weeks. Life is still rudimentary though, and some of the pitfalls can include boredom, basic bathroom/cooking facilities and even the odd snake or spider.

Most of *The Shearers* has been shot in dry and dusty conditions in the back blocks of Australia, areas that many Australians are not familiar with. It is in the faces of the men and women who inhabit the sheds that you can see the stains of a hard-working life. The creases, the eyes and a look of weariness compliment the remoteness of the big sheds to a tee. As a documentary photographer, this is a rich tapestry from which to make photographs.

The images are informative and their honesty provides a real glimpse of what life in remote Australia is all about.

Hughenden Shed, Balranald, NSW

Moolpa Shed, Moulamein, NSW

Pevensey Station, Hay, NSW

Abandoned depot shed near Swan Hill

'When I was a teenager I started walking up the Hume Highway to see what would happen. I arrived in Queensland, and hard work and I became well acquainted.'

John Thomas, retired shearer

The Lakes Shed, Louth, NSW

Still shearing at 85, Frank Buck at Berwick, Vic. in 1983
Facing page: Tasmanian shearer Peter Fish at Toganmain, Hay, NSW

'I'm constantly thinking about me next fishing trip or me next hunting trip or me kids or me wife or whatever the case may be. I'm thinking about how quick I can get home to them and if I work hard then I can spend more time at home.'

Gordon Fehst, shearer

Steve Handley, 'The Chinchilla Killer', averages more than 300 sheep per day
Facing page: Shearer Gordon Fehst, Cooinbil Shed, Coleambally, NSW

Farmer Roger Job, Thollolobo Shed, near Mossgiel, NSW

Cooinbil Shed, Coleambally, NSW

Barcaldine Downs Shed, Barcaldine, Qld

Barcaldine Downs Shed, Barcaldine, Qld

Contractor Andrew Morrison, Cooinbil Shed, Coleambally, NSW

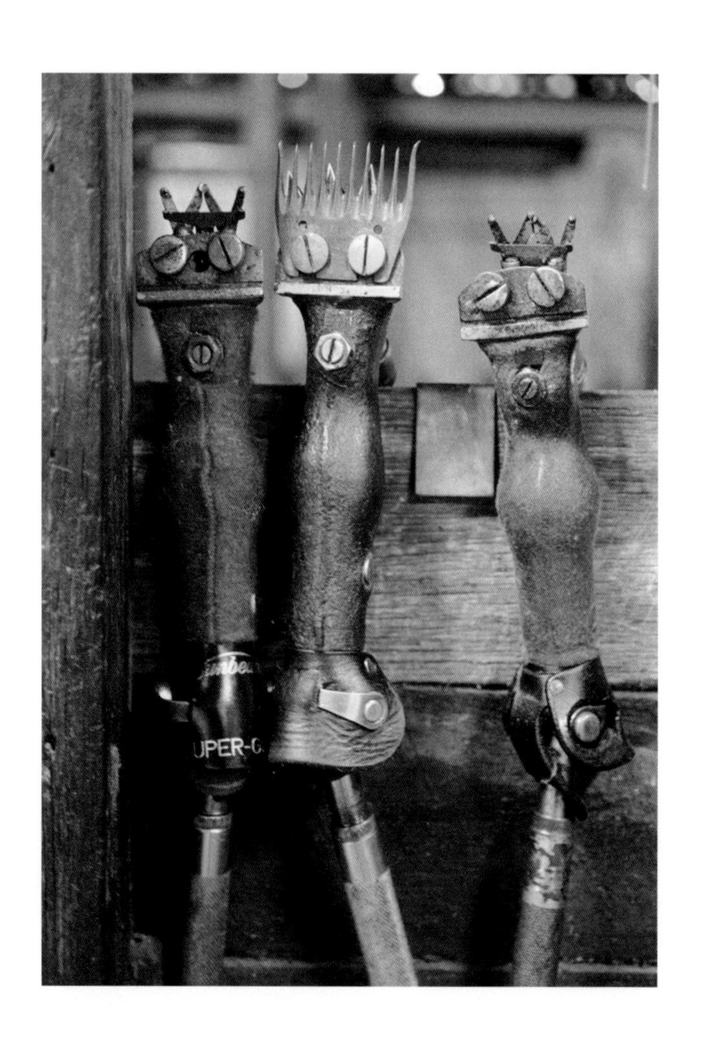

Sharpening cutters at Mooneys Gap, Ararat district, Vic.

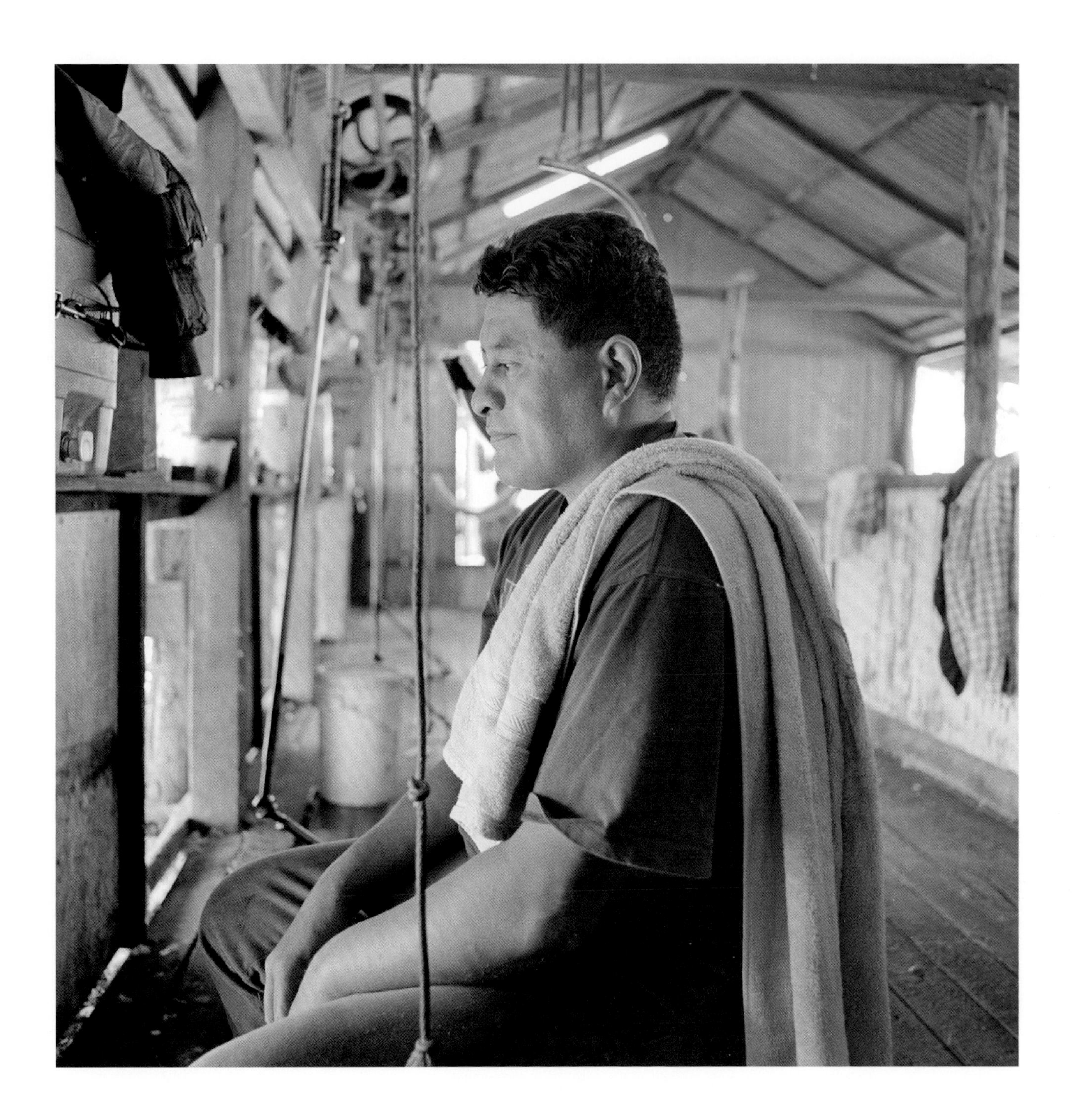

Shearer Bob Tutaki, Flora Glen Shed, Longreach, Qld

'Everyone's there to work as a team. You learn very quickly that if you don't pull your weight, no one else is going to pull it for you.'

Ryan Morrison, shed hand

Hayden Mountjoy, Epsom, Vic.
Facing page: Shearing team at Vale View Shed, near Yass, NSW

Steve Handley, 'The Chinchilla Killer', Bimerah Shed, Longreach, Qld

Almerta Shed, Carrieton, SA

Louth, NSW

Mallawa Shed, near Maude, NSW

Bimerah Shed, Longreach, Qld

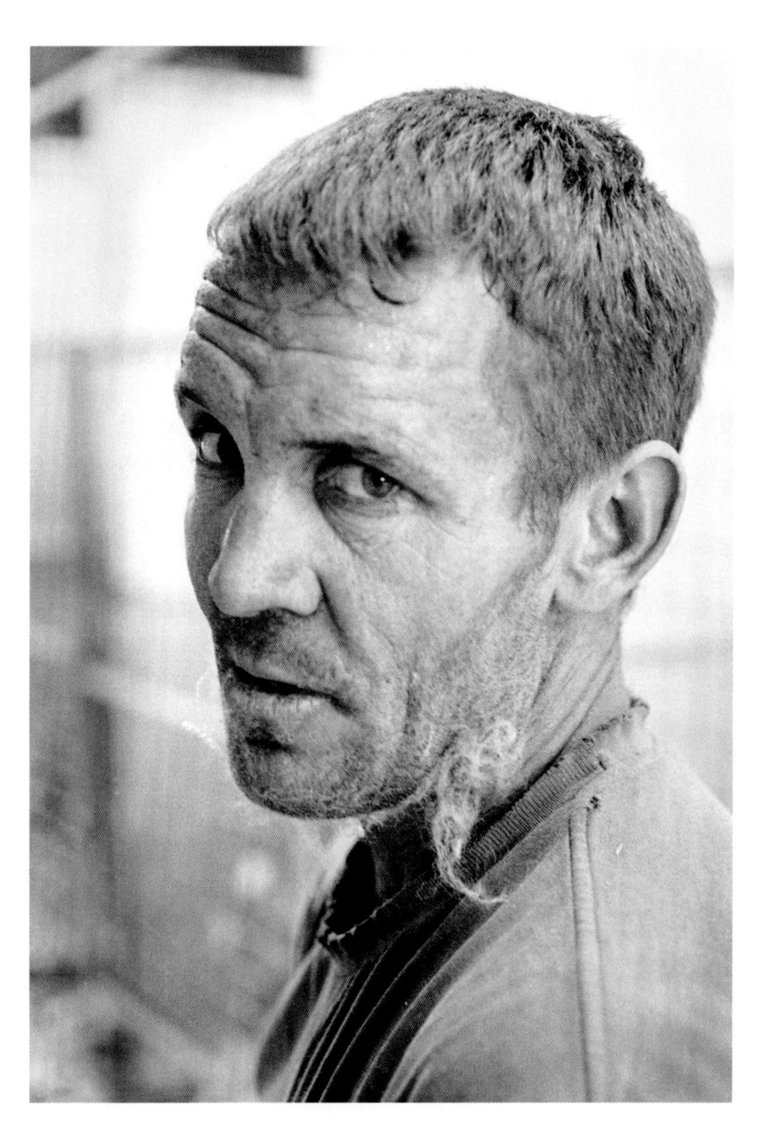

Wool pressers, Cooinbil Shed, Coleambally, NSW

Toganmain, Hay, NSW

Mt Hesse Shed, Winchelsea district, Vic. 1982

Waterbag, Louth, NSW
Facing page: Shearer Bill Hunter, Ulonga Shed, One Tree, NSW

JNO.

Ryan's Shed, Pyalong, Vic. 1976

Eynesbury Shed, Deer Park, Vic. 1981

'It doesn't matter what you have for breakfast, by half past nine you could eat the leg off a chair.'

Barry Wiseman, shearer

Barry Wiseman at Tottington Shed, St Arnaud, Vic.
Facing page: Shearer's cook Judy and her husband Graham Knight, Toganmain, Hay, NSW

Damian Eldridge, Vale View Shed, Yass, NSW

Mt Hesse kitchen, Winchelsea district, Vic. 1985

'The worst meal I had was a chop, about three or four beans, a handful of carrots and a bit of mashed spud.'

Bruce Greenaway, shearer

Yanga kitchen, Balranald, NSW

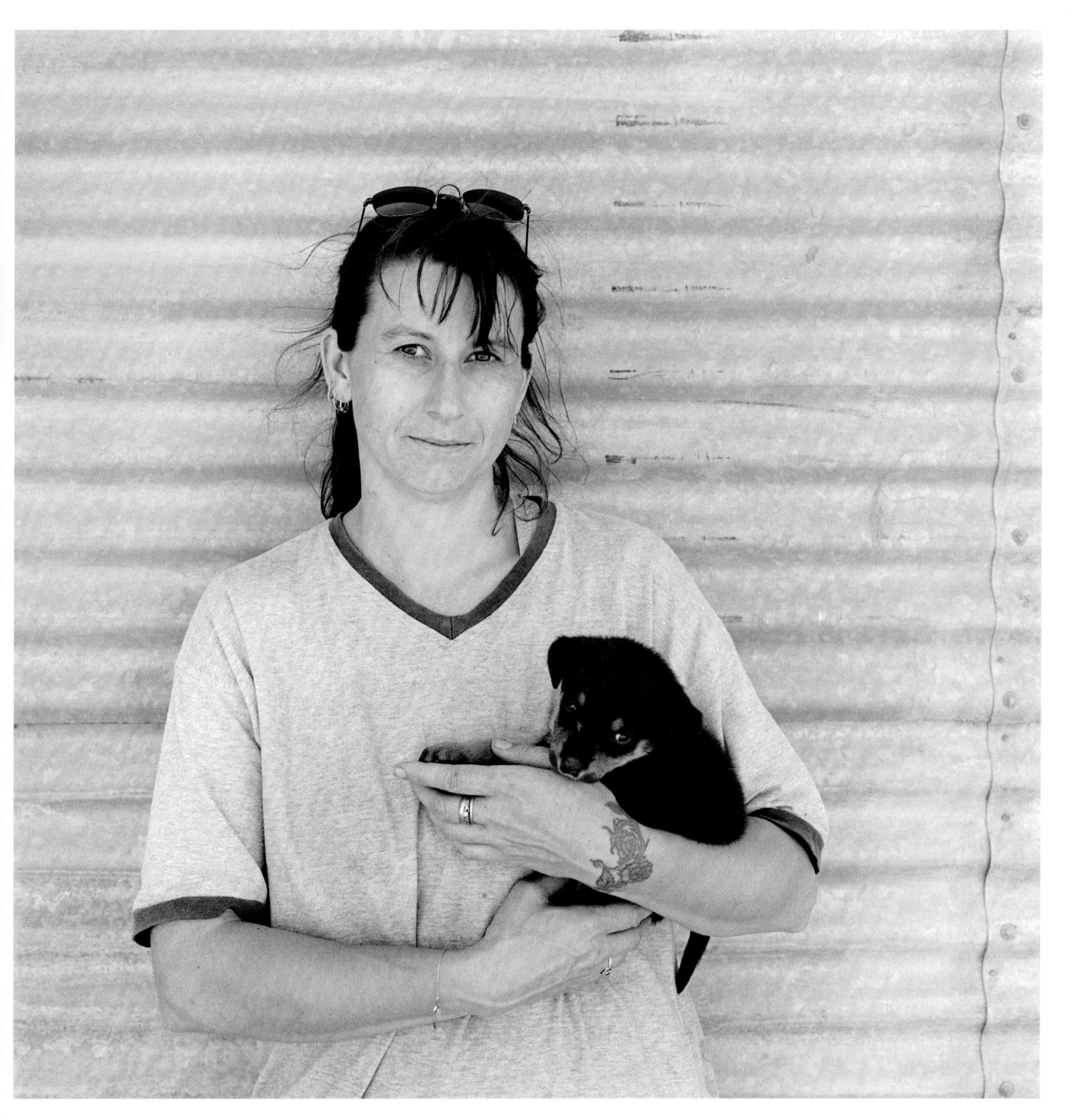

Linda Wright, Maude, NSW

Cooinbil Shed, Coleambally, NSW

Farmer Phil Julian and sons Mark and Andrew,
Annandayle Station, near Holbrook, NSW

NZ shearer John Davis, Cooinbil Shed, Coleambally, NSW

Phil Anesbury and Tom Case: 90 years of shearing between them, Carrieton, SA

Joanne Arkle, Pevensey, Hay, NSW

'A typical morning smoko would be two rounds of sandwiches, and a good sample of cake or slice or whatever was in there, as much as you want.'

Barry Wiseman, shearer

Cooinbil Shed, Coleambally, NSW

GRAEMORE INDUSTRIES
PH. 053 881271

Justin Gee, Maude, NSW
Facing page: Ulonga Shed, One Tree, NSW

The Old Cooinbil Shed, Coleambally, NSW

Hay, NSW

Ian Lilburn, Maude, NSW
Pevensey, Hay, NSW

Toganmain, Hay, NSW
Mt Hesse Station, Winchelsea district, Vic.

Shearers' quarters at The Gums, Burra, SA

Shearer Bernie Constable, Tottington Shed, St Arnaud, Vic.

Learning to shear, Cooinbil Shed, Coleambally, NSW
Facing page: Retired shearer John Thomas, Macclesfield, Vic.

'Back then it was common to learn with a sympathetic shearer who'd allow you finish off the last hind leg and once you'd become proficient at the last hind leg you'd come in a little bit earlier.'

John Thomas, retired shearer

Toganmain, Hay, NSW

Gidgee Shed, Louth, NSW

'Towards the end of the season there'd be some shearers and shed hands who didn't want the shed to end because they didn't have a home. One fellow told me he'd spent Christmas day over at a rabbit burrow waiting for rabbits to come out. He was a gambler and he was flat broke.'

John Thomas, retired shearer

Pevensey Shed, Hay, NSW

Hay, NSW

One Oak Shed, Jerilderie, NSW

Mt Hesse Shed, Winchelsea district, Vic.

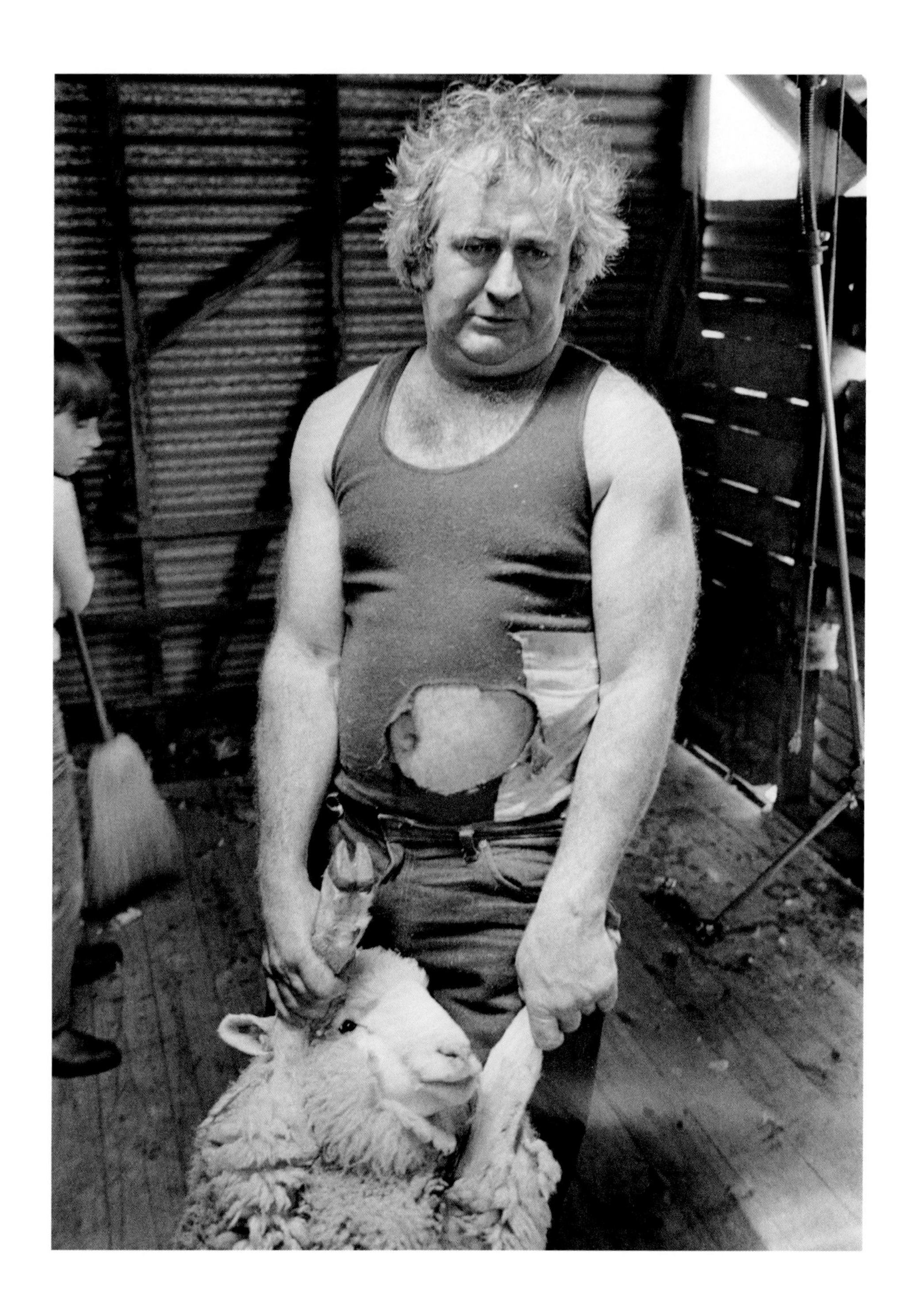

Shearer Eddie Lewis, Buffalo, Vic. 1982

Gidgee Shed team, Louth, NSW

Historic Mungadal Shed, Hay, NSW

Shearers' moccasins on the classer's table

Cooinbil shearers' quarters, Coleambally, NSW

Mt Hesse Shed, Winchelsea district, Vic.

Moolpa Shed, Moulamein, NSW
Facing page: David Hodgkinson, Vale View, Yass, NSW

'I love the land and I love wool and I love sheep.'
Andrew Benn, wool classer

Wool classer Andrew Benn, Cooinbil Shed, Coleambally, NSW

Lionel Matthews and Damian Raudino, Pevensey, Hay, NSW

Linc Storey and Peter Reid, The Springs, Carrieton district, SA

Ulonga Shed, One Tree, NSW

Shearer's backside, Neil Dunstone, Buffalo, Vic, 1982

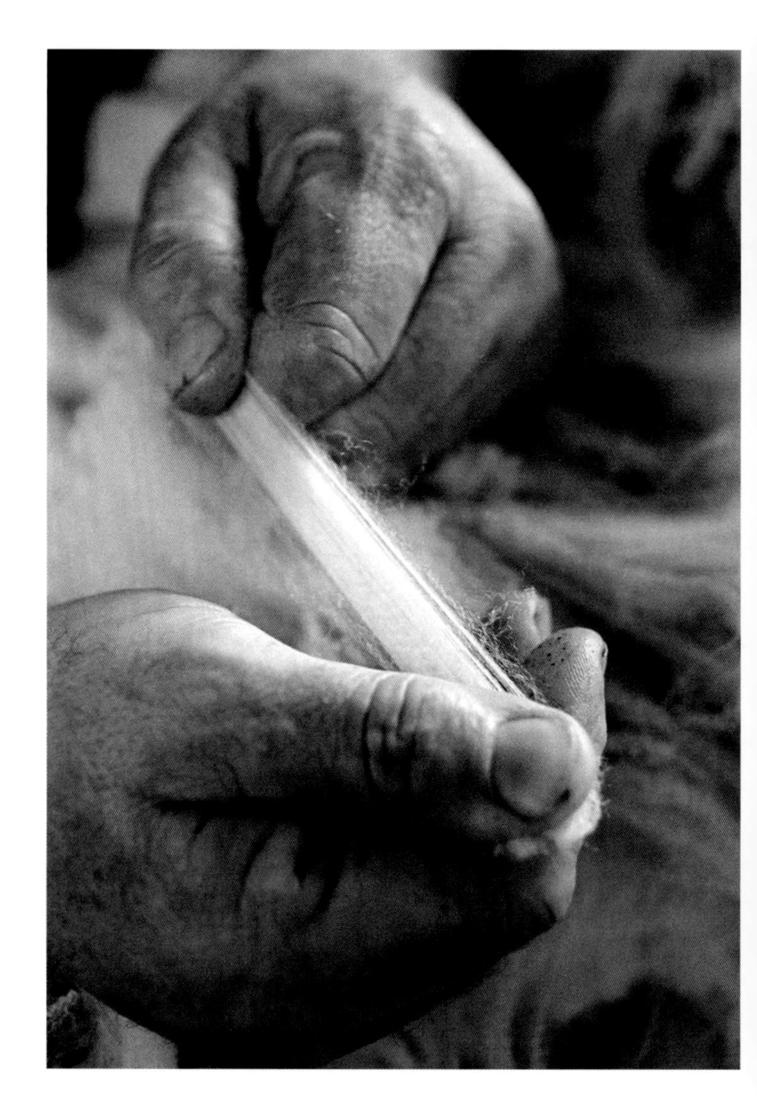

Overseer Glen Richardson, Cooinbil Shed, Coleambally, NSW
Hay, NSW

Shearer Neil Dunstone oiling cutters, Buffalo, Vic. 1982

Comb cleaning, Puckapunyal Shed, Seymour district, Vic.
Facing page: Shearers' cutters

'They tried to ban different types of gear (wide combs), but it was all about New Zealanders shearing in Australia.'

Gordon Fehst, shearer

Blade shearing, Yanga Shed, Balranald, NSW

Blades and oilstone, Yanga Shed, Balranald, NSW

Shearer Sean Cunningham, Cooinbil Shed, Coleambally, NSW

Bill Dobbin, Hazelwood, Vic. 1979

Shearer Brian Gloede, Almerta Station, Carrieton, SA

Peter 'Walkabout' Stewart, Maude, NSW

Field shearing, Hay, NSW

Facing page: Sheep farmers Daryl and Anne Marshall, Moyston, Vic.

WARNING
Valvoline
ANTI-FREEZE, ANTI-BOIL
V-SERIES
PROTECTS ALL METALS
INCLUDING ALUMINIUM
20 LITRES
TWENTY TWO

Shorn, Toganmain, Hay, NSW

Shorn again, Hay, NSW

Maude, NSW

Toilet block at Tin Tin Shed, Balranald, NSW

Anna Lilburn and daughter Lily, Maude, NSW

Louth, NSW

*‘Wherever you go in the back country,
the further you go the better the people get.’*

Fred Lawrie, retired shearer

Retired wool classer Bob Williams (93) and shearer Fred Lawrie (95)
at the final shearing at Yanga Shed, Balranald, NSW

YANGA
LMS CRT
17

Historic Mungadal shearers' quarters, Hay, NSW

Old Ferrier's wool press and Red Gum, Nora Bend, Tooleybuck, NSW

Legendary Isis Downs Shed, Isisford, Qld

The Springs, Carrieton district, SA

Toganmain, Hay, NSW

Mt Hesse Shed, Winchelsea district, Vic.

Roly Desailly, Pevensey Shed, Hay, NSW

Mt Hesse Shed, Winchelsea district, Vic. circa 1983
Facing page: Robbie Johnston in Tarzan singlet, Bimerah Shed, Qld

LANDMAR

Field shearing break, Hay, NSW

Shearer John Taylor, Thollologoy Shed, Mossgiel, NSW

'Grandad was a shearer after the Boer War. He shore with blades. Three hundred-odd a day, three fifty a day was common in those days with blades. Not a bad tally when that's all cut by hand and not by machine.'

Pat Dobbin, shearer

Pat Dobbin, Hazelwood, Vic. 1979

Bill Dobbin's Shed, Hazelwood, Vic.
Facing page: Toganmain Shed, Hay, NSW

IL FILT
DAMS & C

Roustabout Paddy West and wool classer Julieanne Kelly,
Thollolboy Shed, Mossgiel, NSW
Shearer Linc Storey, The Springs, Carrieton district, SA

Roustabout, Bimerah Shed, Longreach, Qld
NZ shearer, Toganmain Shed, Hay, NSW

Roustabouts, Glenhope Shed, Hay, NSW

Shearers' cooks, Cooinbil Station, Coleambally, NSW

Shearer Justin Gee with Caroline and their son Brody,
Uardry Station, Hay, NSW

Eynsbury kitchen, Deer Park, Vic. 1982

Mooneys Gap Shed, Ararat district, Vic.

Butchering lamb in a meat safe

Shearer Chris Weiderman, Hay, NSW

Pevensey Shed, Hay, NSW

'It's not a good place for an attitude.'

Mike Hansby, shearer

NZ shearer, Mike Hansby, Cooinbil Shed, Coleambally, NSW

SWAN
DRAUGHT

Wangarip Shed, Willaura, Vic.

Pyalong, Vic. 1976

Pevensey Shed, Hay, NSW

Barry Wells's damaged shearing hand

'Shearing's taught me how to deal with a lot of pain, taught me how to drink, taught me how to drive long distances when I'm tired and taught me how to work with a mob of people when you're living together for a month on end.'

Ricky Sarre, shearer

Shearer Ricky Sarre, Yanga Shed, Balranald, NSW
Facing page: Boydic Ormond, Mungadal Station, Hay, NSW

Peter 'Walkabout' Stewart, Mallawa Shed, Maude, NSW

Cobran Shed, Hay, NSW

Shed hand Dudley Snow, Flora Glen Shed, Longreach, Qld

Shearer Darryl (Duck) Burns, Louth, NSW

Tom, Jenny and Bryan Small, Tottington Shed, St Arnaud, Vic.
David Houston, Budgewah Shed, Hay, NSW

Bimerah Station, Longreach, Qld

Mossgiel, NSW

Charlie Farrar, farm graveyard, Mossgiel, NSW 2002

Toganmain, Hay, NSW

'It's an awesome feeling when you walk out of the shed and you're absolutely knackered but yet you still feel good about the fact you've worked so hard for the day.'

Gordon Fehst, shearer

Pevensey Station, Hay, NSW

Shearer Mick Lucas, Cooinbil Station, Coleambally, NSW

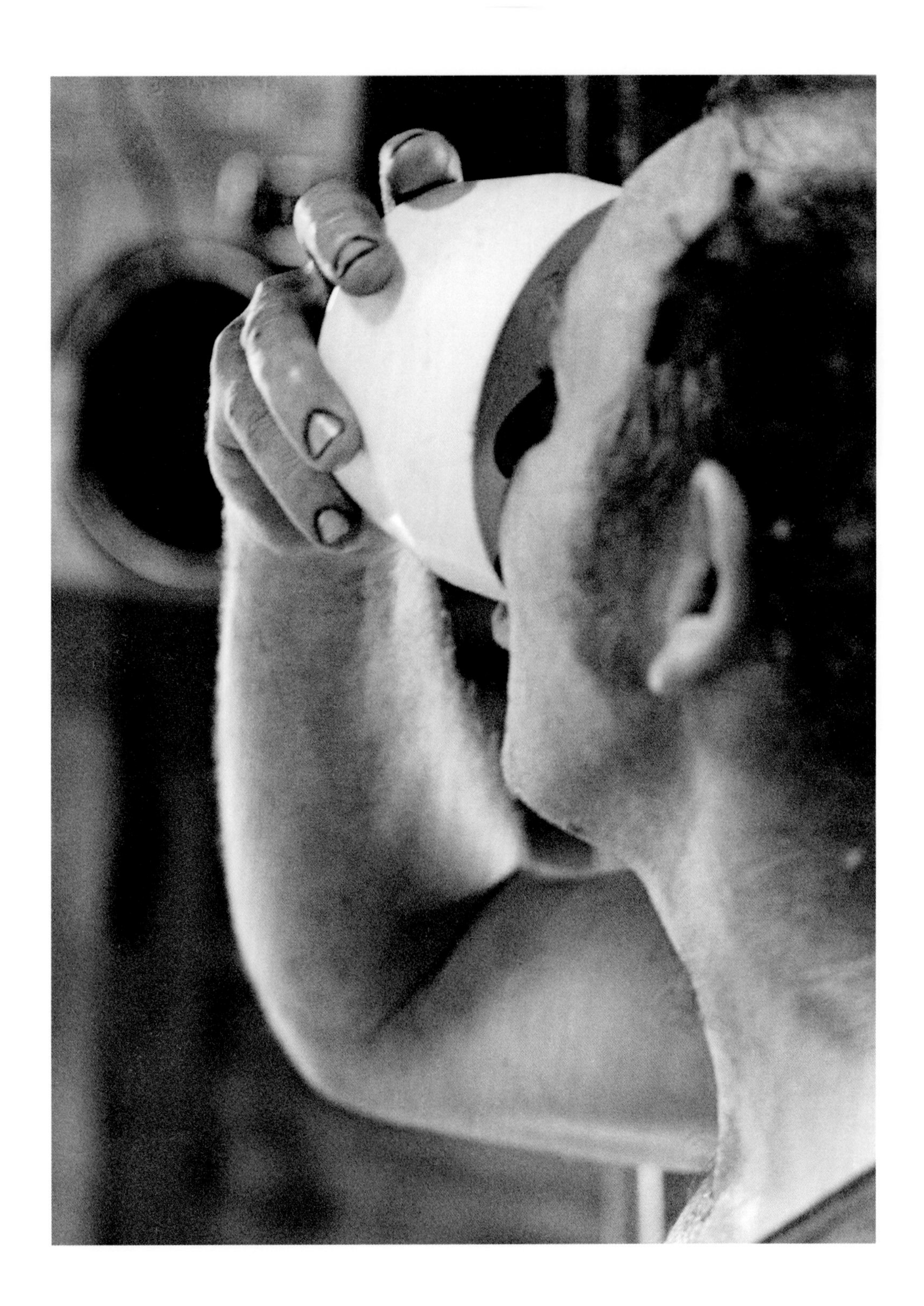

Bray Timmins' Shed, Buffalo, Vic.

Cooinbil Shed, Coleambally, NSW
Facing page: Tess, Tottington Shed, St Arnaud, Vic.

BJ Duncan, Almerta Shed, Carrieton, SA

Louth, NSW

Pyalong, Vic. 1976

Clive Timmins working in his father's shed, Buffalo, Vic. 1982
A raised board, Glenhope Shed, Hay, NSW

Wool classing in the early 1980s, Seymour, Vic.

Hazelwood, Vic.

Shearers' time bell at Habbies Howe Shed, Seymour, Vic.
Facing page: Cooinbil Shed, Coleambally, NSW

'To see some of them battling the pain and how
they nearly crawl off the board at the end of the day,
to see someone put themselves through that
much agony is, I think, quite tragic.'
Enid Black, Hay

Uardry Shed, Hay, NSW

Derek and Chris, Mallawa Shed, Maude, NSW

One Oak Shed, Jerilderie, NSW

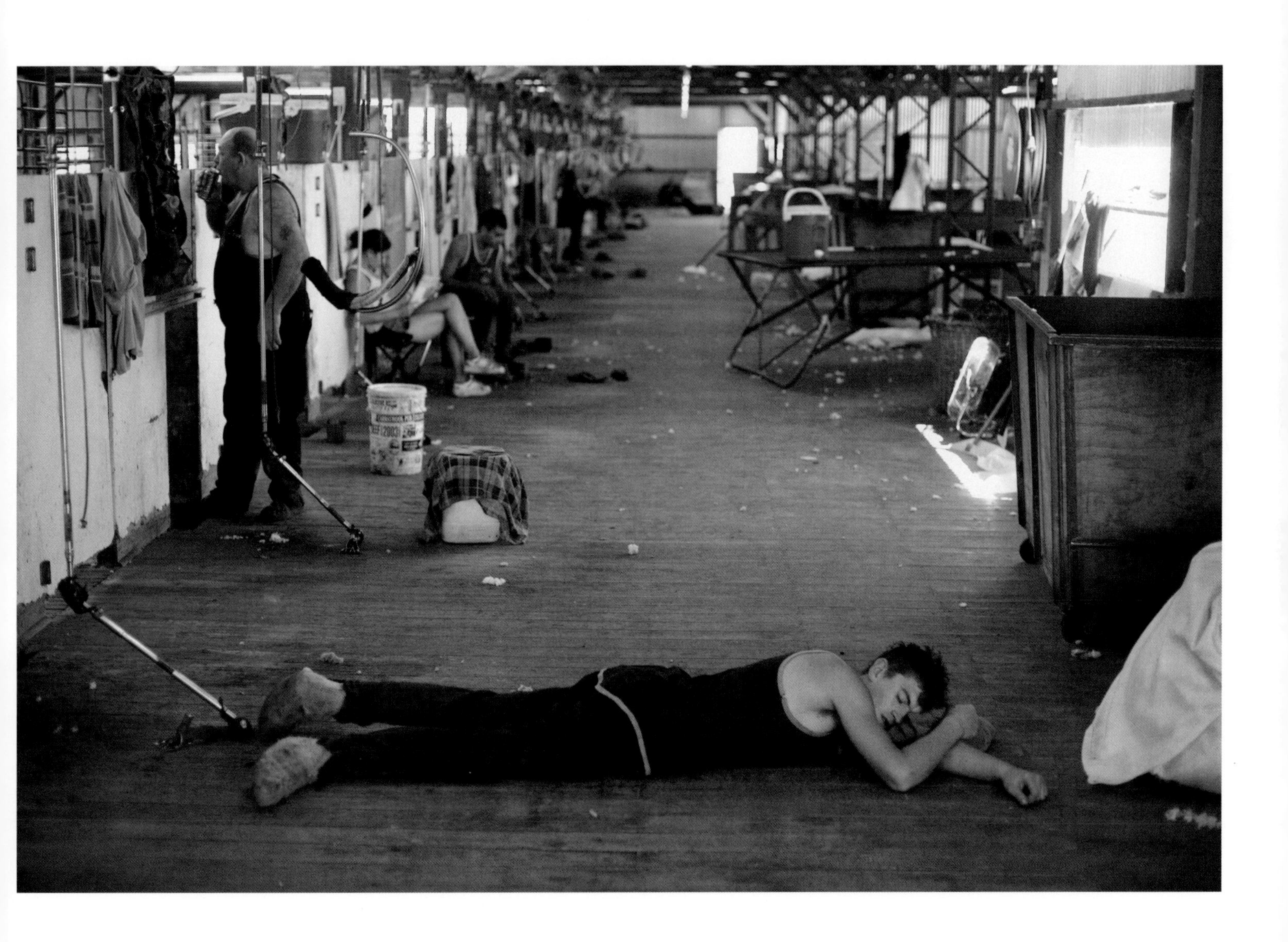

Shearer Shaun Cunningham, Cooinbil Shed, Coleambally, NSW

'We've only ever done one shed apart.
We've pretty much worked together all the time.'
Roustabout Josie and shearer Phil Comitti

PIPING HOT

Doug Allen and Garry Byrne, Thollolоboy Shed, Mossgiel, NSW

Father and son shearers, Mick and Murray Lucas,
Cooinbil Shed, Coleambally, NSW

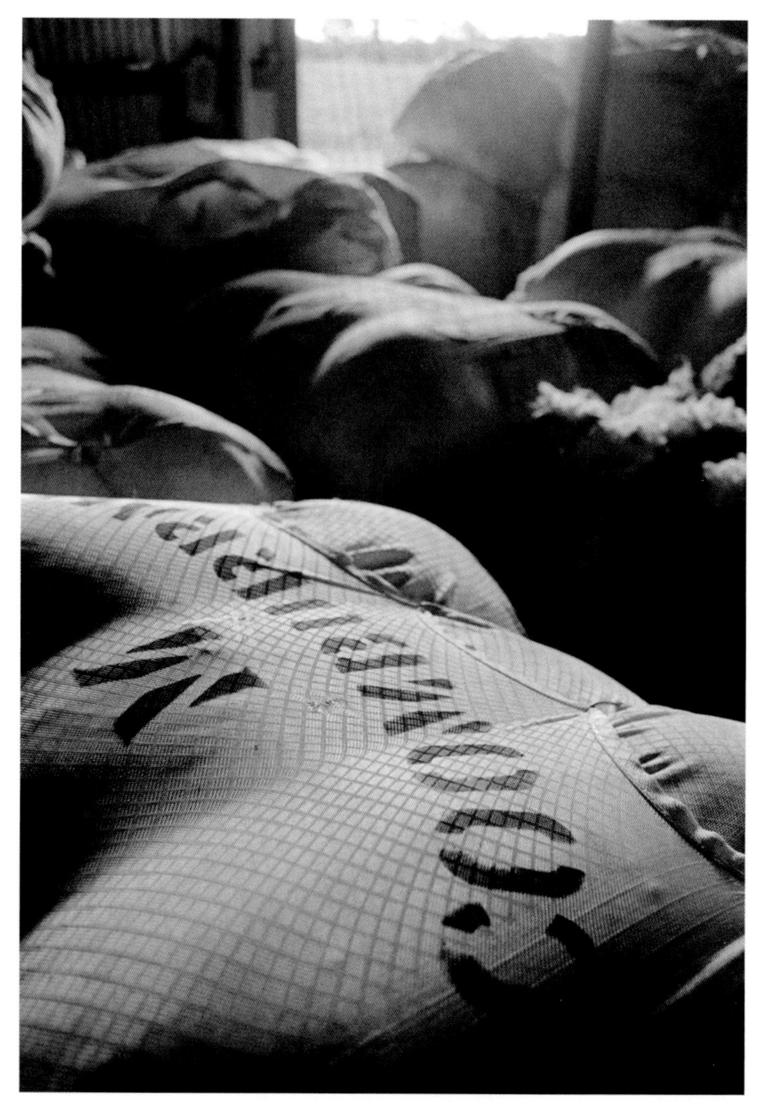

Wool presser's stencils and wool bales

Tolly Bowden's Flora Glen team, Longreach, Qld

Bunga Byrnes, Mungadal Shed, Hay, NSW
Facing page: Ralph Booth, Glenhope Shed, Hay, NSW

Shearing contractor Tolly Bowden, Flora Glen Shed, Longreach, Qld
Shearer Ian Parker, Cobran Shed, Hay, NSW

Pevensey team, Hay, NSW, 2000

Cooinbil Station, Coleambally, NSW

Cooinbil shearers' quarters, Coleambally, NSW

Lake Mungo Shed, Mungo, NSW

Pevensey Shed, Hay, NSW

ACKNOWLEDGEMENTS

I would like to thank the following people for helping me produce this book:

First, my beautiful wife Josie and my children Sarah, Lachlan and Clare for enduring my obsession.

My mother and father John and Betty Chapman for all their efforts in raising and encouraging me.

John Cato, photographer, teacher, friend and mentor for showing me the way.

All the photographic community who believe and have faith in projects such as these, but a special thanks to Michael Silver, Stuart Baker, Robert McGrath, David Marks, Ponch Hawkes, David Johns, Julie Millowick and Peter Eve.

All the shearers, for their interest and their ready acceptance of the importance of the project, especially Peter Stewart, Pat Dobbin, Barry Wiseman, the late Neil Dunstone and John Thomas.

Kaye and Andrew Morrison from National Grazing Services at Hay, NSW, for all the advice, kindness, hospitality and feeds.

Enid Black and Tim Lee for all their contacts, travel guidance, vast knowledge and help.

Jane Scott and all the staff at the Monash Gallery of Art, Mulgrave.

Sara Hector for letting me loose at Hay, and all the staff at 'Shear Outback', the Shearers Hall of Fame at Hay, New South Wales.

Cathy Smith and Magnolia Flora at Lothian Books, Mark Hanlin for helping to choose the photographs and helping to put them in order and Phil Campbell for his beautiful design work.

And finally, to all the farmers and property managers for allowing me access to their properties, especially the Twynam Agricultural Group for allowing me to photograph their beautiful sheds.

TECHNICAL NOTES

Over the last 30 years I have used all sorts of photographic equipment, but by the 1990s had settled into using the following:

Hasselblad 500CM or Cx cameras, mainly with 80mm and 50mm lenses.

Canon EOS 35mm cameras and various lenses.

Canon EOS 1Ds and D20 digital cameras.

Kodak Tri-X film processed in D-76 at 1:1.

The images in the book were scanned from negative on an Imacon Flextite Precision Scanner.

At all times I have let the light do the talking. No flash or reflectors were used in making photos for *The Shearers*.

In the end though, it isn't what's in your hand, but what's in your head, that makes a great photograph.

Images from *The Shearers* can be purchased from the author: printsales@bigcheez.com.au